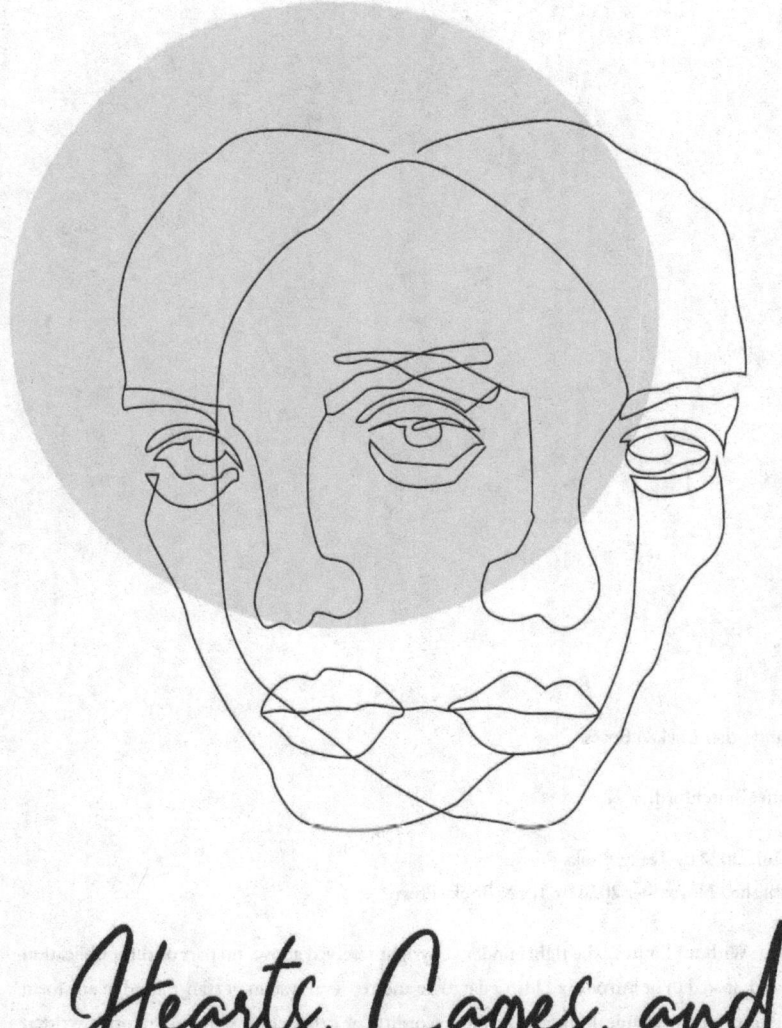

Hearts, Cages, and other Locked Boxes

A. E. Bratchford

Hearts, Cages, and other Locked Boxes

Copyright © Anna Bratchford, 2022

First published July 2022 by Tea & Books Press
This edition published November 2026 by Tea & Books Press

All rights reserved. Without limiting the rights under copyright reserved above, no part of this publication may be reproduced, stored in or introduced into a database and retrieval system or transmitted in any form or any means (electronic, mechanical, photocopying, recording or otherwise) without the prior written permission of both the owner of copyright and the above publishers.

Cover art by Pawan Anjana (@pawananjana2000 on Fiverr)

Cover design for this edition A. E. Bratchford

Internal illustrations by Ifrah Fatima (@fatimaseehar on Fiverr)

ISBN 978-1-7638294-8-0

Hearts, Cages, and other Locked Boxes

A.E. Bratchford

If you are reading this,
then this is for you.

Contents

Introduction   1

The Heart

    Spare Button   7

    Missing Steps   9

    Ace of Hearts   10

    With All My Heart   13

    Companionship   15

    Unrequited   17

    Truth   19

The Cage

    The Self   23

    Let Me Out   25

    Wistful Stranger   26

    Fog   29

    Scream   31

The Lock

    Sleepless   34

    Voices   37

Mapmaker	39
Choking Hazards	41
Sunset	43
The Key	
Soul in a Locket	46
Alive	48
Winding Path	51
The Wall	52
Unsung	55
Dragon	56
Afterword	61
Acknowledgements	62
About the Publisher	65
Also Published by Tea & Books Press	67

Introduction

These poems have been written over quite a number of years, spanning back to about 2015, and now, as a collection, they are a tribute to how much I have progressed both with myself and in my writing. These poems are a timeline, and a progression of growth. I am proud of every single word you are about to read. I hope you find something for yourself in these words, as I found something in writing them.

For this reprint in hardcover, I reached out to someone to illustrate my collection of poems. It is something I had been thinking about doing in the early stages of originally publishing this collection, but at that point there was so much to the process of self-publishing that I didn't want to add something else for me to worry about. In the past few years, however, I have learnt a lot, and am so excited to bring this illustrated edition of Hearts, Cages, and other Locked Boxes to you. I hope you love it as much as I do!

I'm drawn towards rainbows
all those colours

marching

marching

what sin have I done?
to need to prove
my right to love

was I wired wrong?
did red go into blue
and blue hang loose?

please answer me this

what am I?

The Heart

Spare Button

I'm the odd one out
you chose to keep
just left aside
for when you need

a fix me up
for empty plans
when things didn't go quite right

I'm a stand in
when your threads unstitch
or when your bindings
start to fray

they say I shouldn't
that you're using me
that I'm just a spare button

but I'm your spare button

you see?

Missing Steps

Unrequited love
feels like
missing a step

whether you're falling up
or down

you only realise
once it's too late

and it hurts

oh,
it hurts

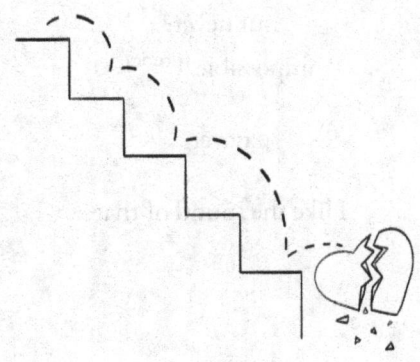

Ace of Hearts

I walk this world
you, me the same

two arms
two legs

one foot first
then the next

I'm just like you
I say

but
they say not

all the time?
far too much ^(slut)

but never?
impossible ^(prude)

never

I like the sound of that

perhaps
almost never

full hearts
and empty beds

Ace of Hearts

that's me

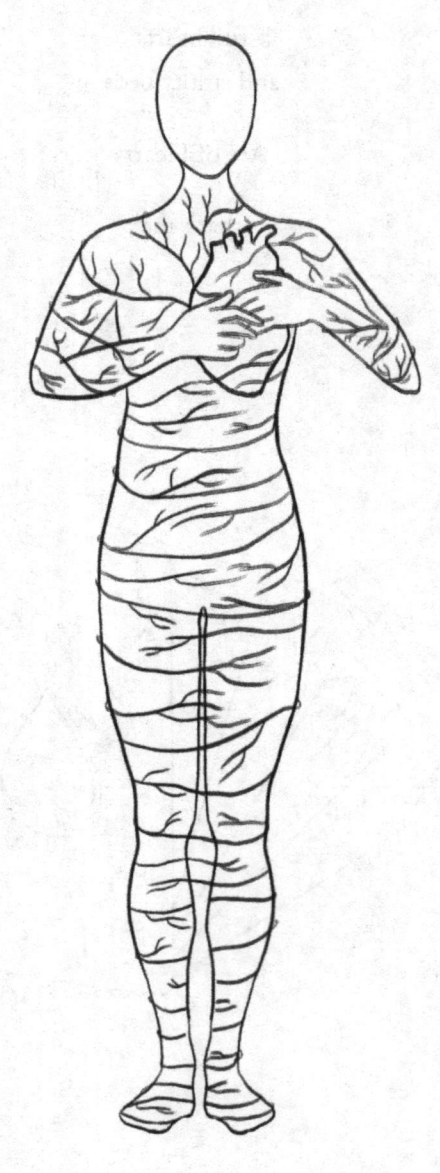

With All My Heart

I care
I care a lot
I care too much

distance is no barrier
through screen
through page
through life

endless worlds
endless words
endless lives

I live them all
the love and the heartbreak
the ineffable joy

I feel it too
every last bit

I care
I care a lot
with all my heart

Companionship

I will stay with you,
My love; through the longest day,
And the darkest night.

Unrequited

My love
it feels like an age
since I've seen you

your eyes
your lips
your hair

for you
no time has passed at all

you don't notice
while I-
I notice too much

please just
see me
as I see you

Truth

This truth
in all its forms
presents like a block of chocolate

enticing
with a promise of paradise
a promise of sanctuary

telling this truth
with no foreseeable calm
is like eating the last cube

no bliss
no satisfaction
no joy in that sweet familiarity

just churning
aching
guilt

that something once so pure
so precious
is gone for good

because I thought that maybe
just maybe

she'd want to share the chocolate too

The Cage

The Self

how can they know me?
when I do not know myself;
first prize for knowledge.

Let Me Out

This form of mine
it's not a body

in truth
it is
a

|c|a|g|e|

let
me
out
let
me
out

Let Me Out

Wistful Stranger

Empty names
and empty faces
mysterious sights
with peculiar graces

I pass by
a stranger
in someone else's world

their familiarities
their everyday humdrum
more than I could ever see from here
from the outside

to me
a mystery

to them
they know the streets
the alleys
all those sorts of nooks and crannies

where she found that five dollar note
where he had his first kiss
where the twins used to ride their bikes

to me all unknown
but they're there
those little stories

the ones which make us human
joining all the puzzle pieces
to bring a place to life

they will show themselves in time

with patience
with love
with care

so maybe
just maybe

I'll find my place there too

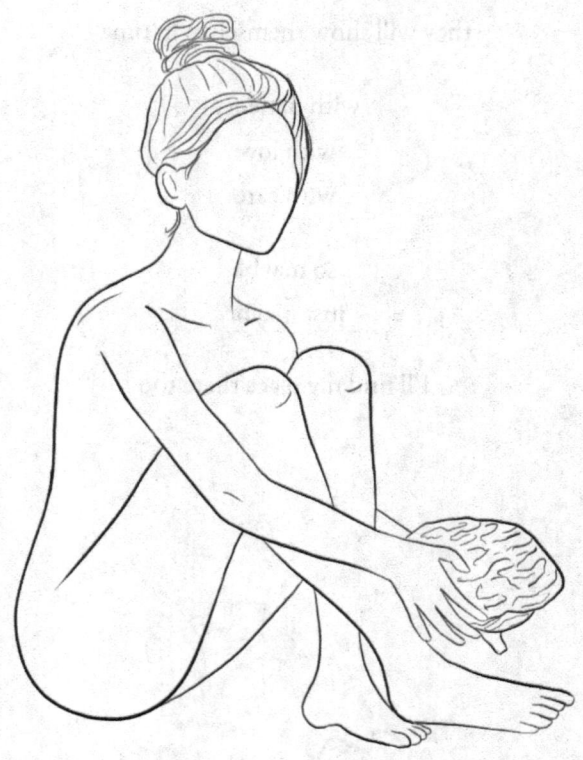

Fog

Brain fog
like static
it sparkles

Loud
Dull

it fills my mind
crowds my senses

Filing
Pressing
Grating away

Scream

Skin deep, not enough
not even the soul would do

that unearthly sound

through my layered walls it dug

until it had
carved
me
out

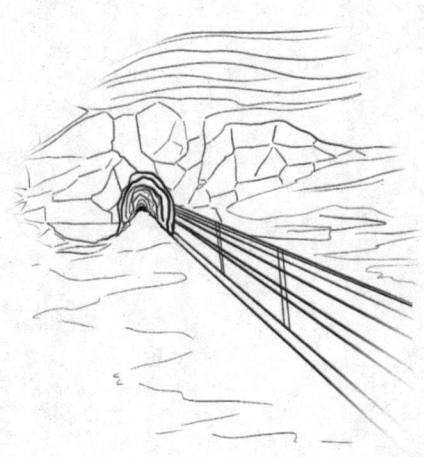

The Lock

Sleepless

There are storm clouds
overhead

residing in my head
too

Waiting
Baiting

one day
maybe
they'll let me rest

until then
they try their best
to not

when will they let me sleep?
let me dream

you
storm clouds

overhead
in my head

please

let
me
dream

Voices

Do not listen
in these hours

the lonely time
between 10pm
and 5am

do not listen
to the pointed nothings
whispered
carefully in your mind

the last you think
before you sleep
and the first as you wake

alone
but not

quiet
but not

Do not listen
Do not listen
Do not listen

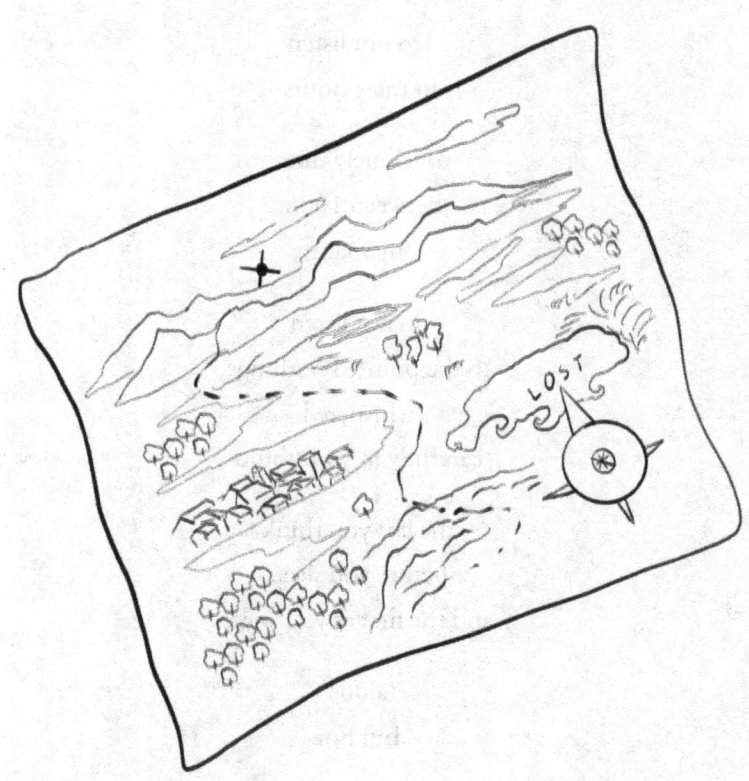

Mapmaker

They tell me things I don't believe
of someone I don't know

I do my best to find them
buried deep inside

no matter how far down I dig

No kind
Or strong
Or fair

I hate this map to nowhere
no little red X in sight
not hidden in the symbols
no key to ease my plight

so I sit here swinging
between the me you know
and the me I found inside
not ever landing still

I wish there was a manual
to tell me who I am
it might just stop this swinging
and give me time to land

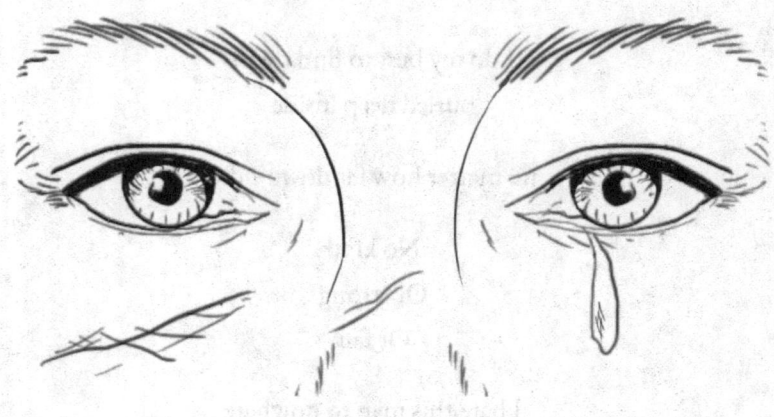

Choking Hazards

Tears choke
much in the same way
fingers can

slowly
at first
then all at once

they leave burning
eyes
throat

an ache in my chest
I can't quite let go

tears
blotch red
soon to be invisible

fingers
they bruise
black and blue

Sunset

The sunset catches
those silver giants
with a shine that stings

nothing like the warmth
that floods the fields
back home

Dorothy said
there's no place like home

she was right

some days all I want
all I need
is to click my heels together

once twice thrice

to be back in open fields
as far as the eye can see

The Key

Soul in a Locket

How shall I use these broken wings
when to fix them
I must pluck the feathers
from another's back

I cannot bring a second here
to be beat
and broken
too

but as time ebbs on
my mask will fall

I'll need a little help

to let someone in
past my façade
my lies and smiles

all to gain a way
to find myself a cure

an elixir
for normality

no need to wait
with bated breath
heart thudding painfully
within my chest

for a steady hand
the driest palm

to lose that gnawing doubt

we'd chip away the layers
let the casing fall away

leaving a renewed
and confident
soul

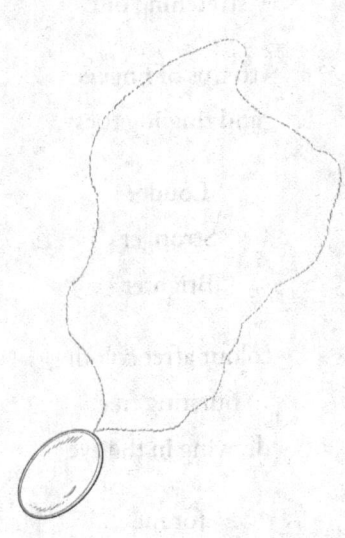

Alive

Unexpected
starting in my chest

small
hesitant
bubbling

the feeling grows

filling down
stretching out

to tips of fingers
and tingling toes

Louder
Stronger
Brighter

colour after colour
bursting free
drawing in the eye

for me
you make me better
than the darkness
in my mind

laughter
thank you

for helping me
be me

Winding Path

Roads
that lead to
recovery of self
are tough at the best of times-
but friend, if you persevere
you'll come out stronger
than before-
brave

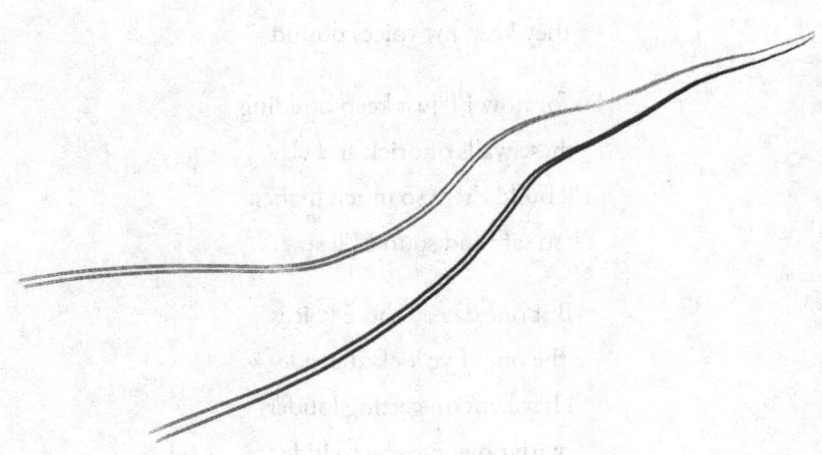

The Wall

Sometimes things just happen
much bigger than can be
They cause me now to wonder
if those things would crumble me

If those walls I built are strong enough
if they're built from stone or sand
If just one move will crush them
or strong they'll silently stand

These walls may keep the voices out
they may keep me safe and sound
But like all walls they have two sides
they keep my voices bound

So for now I'll just keep building
these walls of brick and clay
I'll build them so much higher
so safe and sound I'll stay

But one day all those voices
the ones I've locked inside
They kept on getting louder
with nowhere else to hide

Time to find a door then
to get one of us out

I'm not quite sure I built one
none, without a doubt

But that's when I hear a click
an all familiar voice
They've made their own bright doorway
they offer me a choice

I stand here with a mallet now
to knock through all these walls
With one hit nothing happens
with the second one brick falls

With every piece that crumbles down
I open up my heart
With every hit I wonder
Should I have done this from the start?

Unsung

There is nothing sweeter
Than the sound of chorused voice
All pulled together gently
Each single note a choice

From there we have you captured
With the gentle strings of song
To draw out all your wonder
Your soul it won't be long

But then there is a moment
Our melodies withheld

We breathe a careful silence
Then reach again for more

We grasp a note still moving
From beyond our silent store
It crouches there so patient
Just waiting there to soar

So our melody continues
Your mind still cradled close
Those unsung notes we foster
The ones remembered most

Dragon

Harshest comments
cutting words anew
you think I don't hear them

Hidden bruises
more than skin deep
you think I don't see them

But you are me and I am you
By now we should know better

I should burn you to the ground
To walk among the ashes
I must leave my soul behind
I must become my dragon

just believing
took its toll
I tore myself apart

leaving just a shell behind
just my hollow heart

Laughter lost
those quiet looks
how could I still not notice?

For you are me and I am you
I now should know you better

I should burn you to the ground
To walk among the ashes
I must leave my soul behind
I must become my dragon

with every word of kindness here
and every tender touch

I picked my wings up
piece by piece
and now
I'm soaring free

So,
Anna

I did burn you to the ground
I walked among your ashes
I scooped my soul up at the gate
I now don't need my dragon

Afterword

Thank you so much for reading my journey of growth and self-understanding through this poetry collection. Like I mentioned in my introduction to this collection. These poems have been written over quite a length of time, so while this collection was quite small, the journey it depicts has been gradual and over a long period of time. So I love being able to see changes in myself and my understanding of who I am through this collection, and I hope you have found something in it too.

If you did enjoy this collection or find something for yourself in my words, please think about leaving a rating or review on whichever site you purchased this, or on Goodreads (or anywhere you usually talk about what you are reading). Reviews and word of mouth are pure gold to indie authors, as they rely on readers along with their own marketing for their books to reach the right audiences. This is the best way you support your favourite indie authors, plus I truly appreciate every review or share of my writing!

Thank you again, I really do appreciate you taking a chance on my collection of poetry.

Acknowledgements

I've always loved reading the acknowledgments pages in a novel. Seeing the support and love behind these authors is amazing; and with my poetry collection, it's no different. This collection has been a long time coming. I recently discovered the earliest poem from this collection is from some time in 2015, back when I was at university. So, from that first poem, until now, I have quite a few people to thank.

First, of course, thank you to my family. Without their love and support, I would never have got to a point where I feel confident enough in myself to actually persevere with this project and get it to this point. As well as my family, thank you to my closest friends. You keep me going.

Thank you so much to Ifrah Fatima over on Fiverr who did the beautiful illustrations for this collection. I absolutely love what she has done to bring so much more life to my words. I can tell she took a lot of time and care with her idea and creativity. I hope you've loved them as much as I do.

I also want to thank Pawan Anjana from over on Fiverr, my cover designer and artist. He did such a gorgeous job with the cover, especially with how I had very little idea of what I wanted for it. He managed to bring me a cover for my poetry collection that I think fits beautifully. As this collection has a plain cover I still wanted to honour his work by printing it as the inside cover.

To my wonderful ARC readers, thank you so much. I really appreciate you and your love for this little collection before it had made it into the world. You guys are amazing!

To the various writing groups I have written with, both online and in person, thank you. You all have been so lovely to write with over the years.

And to anyone who has ever shown any interest in my writing, you have helped me to get to this point, so thank you. I am ever so grateful.

Tea & Books Press is a Naarm/Melbourne, Australia based press that publishes books focused on LGBTQIA+ stories. We love books perfect to curl up with on a rainy day with a hot cuppa and your favourite blanket.

website: www.teaandbookspress.com.au

instagram: @teaandbookspress

email: enquiries@teaandbookspress.com.au

Also Published by Tea & Books Press

From Me to You: Anthology of Human Connections

by

Curated by A. E. Bratchford

Edited by Laura from Hummingbird Editing

With stories and poetry from Avrah C. Baren, A. E. Bratchford, Tess Carletta, Avery Carter, Aimee Donnellan, R. P. Dunwater, H. M. Evans, Noah Hawthorne, Taylor Hubbard, Jaydell, H. L. Moore, Meaghan O'Connor, Hope Swan, and Jake Vanguard

Every day we make new connections, whether it is intentional or not. It is human nature to seek out those connections and nurture them.☐

'From Me to You' features 14 wonderful authors who have all contributed a short story to the theme of connections.

Sink into intricate worlds and the lives of characters who are reaching out, just trying to find their people.

Before She Forgot: A Collection of Vignettes in Verse

by

A. E. Bratchford

Go back in time through the lives of the crew of the Starship L.O.L.A before they became the crew you know.

Before She Forgot includes verse from the perspective of each member of the crew as moments their life lead them towards becoming a member of Tahlia's crew. Read verses of love, loyalty, heartbreak, and eventually that of found family and home.

A home that is torn through by the near loss of life of a crew member - something that changes their life, and the lives of the crew, forever.

With Love, the Stars

by

A. E. Bratchford & T. W. Night

> "Tell me the story
> about how the Sun
> loved the Moon so much,
> she died every night
> to let her breathe."

'With Love, the Stars' is a collection of queer short stories and poems within the genres of romance and sci-fi/fantasy.

Each piece has been lovingly crafted by two authors separately, but then woven together into the words within. A cup of dreams, a few litres of emotion, and of course, a gallon of love has been poured into this collection in the process of its creation.

So if you are looking for stories of love - whether it be new or rekindled, from rivalry to love at first sight, or even stories in worlds and galaxies far beyond our own - you may just find it here amongst the love of the stars.

Forget Me Not: A Sapphic Sci-fi Verse Novel

by

A. E. Bratchford

Beatrice, a lonely traveller, floats through unknown territory in space. Trapped in a survival pod, she has no clue how she ended up there and little memory of much else. All the while, she is haunted by the ghost of someone she feels she should know.

On the other side of the galaxy, a crew of space marauders have almost given up hope of finding the missing member of their crew. One lost in an accident that nearly cost the team more than just their friend.

That being said,
one refuses to accept the truth.

Jordan will stop at nothing to get her friend back but as time goes on, she quickly realises that finding Beatrice was the easy part. What comes next is something she never could have anticipated.

www.ingramcontent.com/pod-product-compliance
Lightning Source LLC
Chambersburg PA
CBHW012054280426
43661CB00119B/1492/J